ANIMAL SUPERPOWERS

AMAZING ANIMAL SURVIVORS

John Townsend

www.raintreepublishers.co.uk
Visit our website to find out
more information about
Raintree books.

To order:
☎ Phone 0845 6044371
▤ Fax +44 (0) 1865 312263
▣ Email myorders@raintreepublishers.co.uk

Customers from outside the UK please telephone +44 1865 312262

Raintree is an imprint of Capstone Global Library Limited,
a company incorporated in England and Wales having its
registered office at 7 Pilgrim Street, London, EC4V 6LB –
Registered company number: 6695582

Text © Capstone Global Library Limited 2013
First published in hardback in 2013
The moral rights of the proprietor have been asserted.

Edited by Rebecca Rissman, Dan Nunn,
  and Catherine Veitch
Designed by Joanna Hinton-Malivoire
Picture research by Mica Brancic
Production by Victoria Fitzgerald
Originated by Capstone Global Library
Printed and bound in China by CTPS

ISBN 978 1 406 24120 4
16 15 14 13 12
10 9 8 7 6 5 4 3 2 1

British Library Cataloguing in Publication Data
Townsend, John
Amazing animal survivors. -- (Animal superpowers)
591-dc23
A full catalogue record for this book is available from the
British Library.

Acknowledgements
We would like to thank the following for permission
to reproduce photographs: Alamy pp. 10 (© Robert
Shantz), 14 (© Design Pics Inc/Jack Goldfarb); Corbis p.
27 (Reuters/© Handout); FLPA pp. 6 (Sunset), 17 (S & D
& K Maslowski); Getty Images pp. 4 (Digital Vision/Peter
Richardson), 8, 9 (Oxford Scientific/Kathie Atkinson),
Nature Picture Library p. 5 (© Jeff Rotman); Photolibrary
pp. 13 (Animals Animals/Raymond Mendez), 26 (Oxford
Scientific (OSF)/Satoshi Kuribayashi); Photoshot p. 12 (©
UPPA/Newcom/ Rodger Mallison); Science Photo Library
pp. 11 (TOM MCHUGH), 15 (KENNETH H. THOMAS),
21 (ALEXIS ROSENFELD); Shutterstock pp. 7 (Gentoo
Multimedia Ltd), 16 (© Stacy Barnett), 18 (© Cigdem
Sean Cooper), 18 (© Mike Bauer), 19 (© Leagam), 20 (©
photobank.kiev.ua), 22 (© Eugene Sim), 23 (© Jonpaul
Hosking), 24 (© Holly Kuchera), 25 (© Geoffrey Kuchera),
29 (© David Grigg).

Cover photograph of emperor penguins with chicks,
Antarctica reproduced with permission of Photolibrary
(Peter Arnold Images/Fritz Polking).

Every effort has been made to contact copyright holders
of material reproduced in this book. Any omissions will
be rectified in subsequent printings if notice is given to
the publisher.

We would like to thank Michael Bright for his invaluable
help in the preparation of this book.

Some words are shown in bold, **like this**. You can find
out what they mean by looking in the glossary.

Contents

Animals can be superheroes!

To be a superhero, you must stay alive with danger all around you. Many animals have secret super-**defences** to keep them safe from harm when danger strikes. Read this book to find out which animals use superpowers to survive.

An octopus pumps out ink to cloud the water, so it can sneak away!

5

Super cool

The **Antarctic** is the coldest and windiest place on Earth. It is far colder than the inside of any freezer! Even so, some birds survive here. Thousands of emperor penguins huddle together to keep warm. They take turns standing on the outside of the group to protect others from icy blasts.

Did you know?
A penguin's feathers and layers of fat keep out the cold.

Super hot

Frogs must keep their skin damp or they will die. This can be difficult in the hottest, driest part of Australia. In Australia, the water-holding frog fills up with water when it rains. Then it buries itself for months underground.

When it rains again, the water-holding frog wakes up and pops out for a refill.

Super dry

All living things need water to survive. But in a super-dry desert, animals need superpowers to live without drinking. Kangaroo rats do not get much **moisture** from the seeds they eat. They have special **kidneys** that reuse their body moisture so they hardly ever need to drink.

Did you know?
Kangaroo rats can jump almost 3 metres to escape danger. That's as far as 15 footballs in a row!

Super defence

Some animals seem to use superpowers to defend themselves when a **predator** strikes. A horned lizard can puff up its body to twice its normal size. This makes it look like a spiny balloon. Then comes the next super weapon … it shoots blood from its eyes! This confuses any predator.

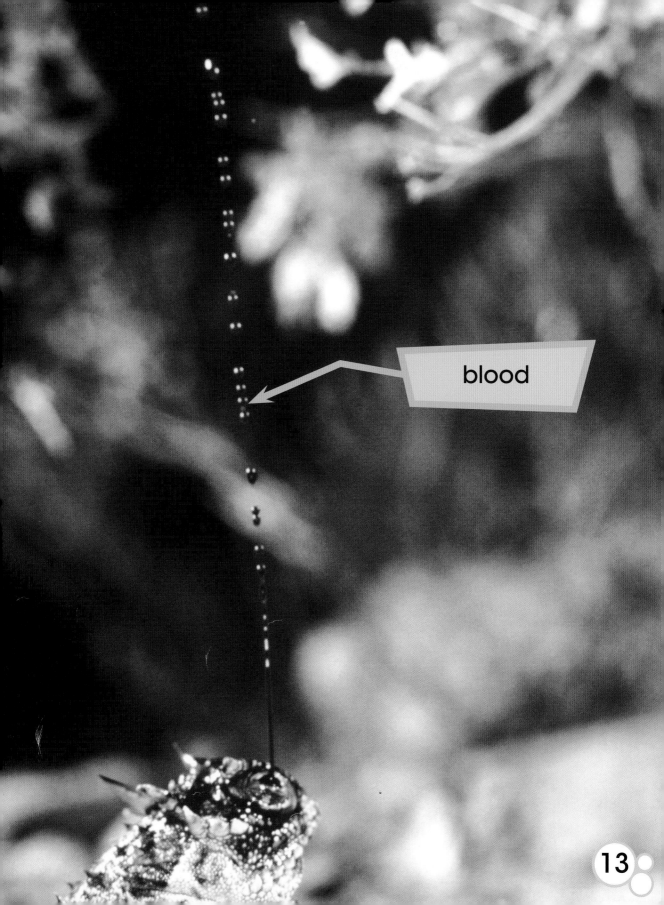

blood

13

Super act

If a hungry **predator** wants to eat you, what can you do? Some animals pretend to be dead and smell rotten. The hognose snake flips on its back with its mouth open and gives off a foul smell to make a predator think it is dead.

Super tricks

When an opossum feels threatened, it plays dead by flopping over, with its eyes closed or staring blankly. It sticks out its tongue, dribbles, and leaks foul-smelling liquid from its bottom. It's best to leave it alone!

After the dog attacked it, this opossum played dead. This saved the opossum's life.

Super scary

The puffer fish may look like a tasty snack to a **predator**. But be warned – this fish has a stretchy stomach that lets it gulp in water and puff up like a spiky ball.

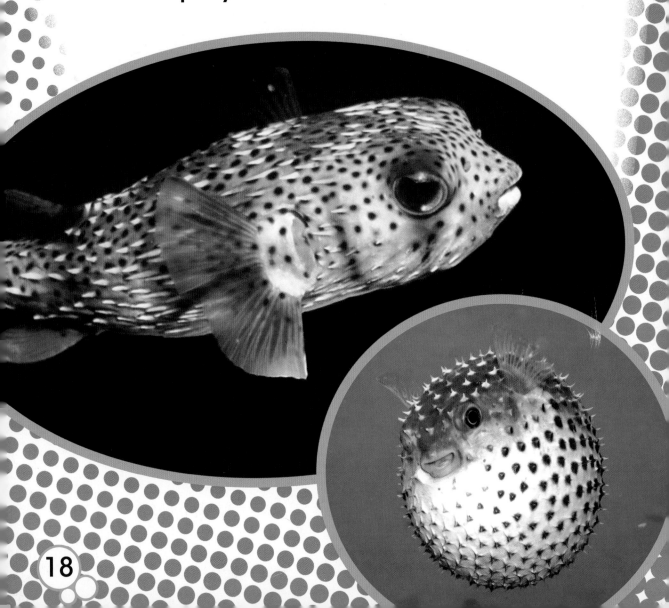

Did you know?

Beware of ever swallowing a puffer fish. It contains deadly **poison** – enough to kill 30 adult humans.

Super limbs

Some animals have the superpower of growing new body parts. Losing a leg for this salamander is nothing to worry about … it just grows a new one! In a fight, a salamander may also **shed** its tail to escape.

new arm

This starfish
is growing a
new arm.

Super disguise

Would you like to become **invisible**? Some animals can seem to disappear! They change colour or shape to become almost totally **camouflaged**.

If it is disturbed from the seabed, a flounder fish flaps away and throws up a cloud of sand. It then settles back to becoming invisible again.

Did you know?
This hard-to-spot stonefish has **poisonous** spines that can kill humans.

Super stink

A great way to defend yourself against an attacker is to fire out foul-smelling liquid from your bottom! Skunks shoot out disgusting and hard-to-remove spray.

The skunk turns round to blast a stinky mist of oily liquid from under its bushy tail.

Super squirt

The bombardier beetle is an insect with a scary weapon. When attacked by a **predator**, this African beetle sprays smelly, boiling **acid**, like a fiery stun gun.

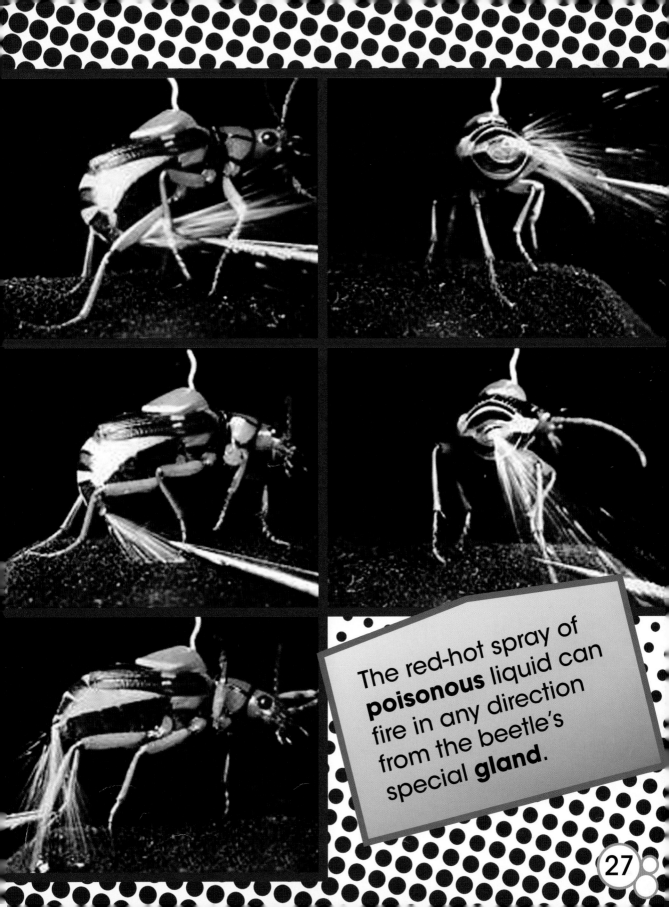

The red-hot spray of **poisonous** liquid can fire in any direction from the beetle's special **gland**.

Quiz: Spot the superhero!

Test your powers of observation and see if you can spot the superhero. You can find the answers on page 32 if you are really stuck!

1. Which of these animals can squirt ink?
a) an octopus
b) a skunk
c) a lizard

2. Which of these animals can shoot blood from its eyes?
a) a snake
b) a horned lizard
c) an opossum

3. Which of these animals can play dead?
a) a hognose snake
b) a kangaroo rat
c) a penguin

4. Which of these animals can swell up to look scary?
a) a beetle
b) a frog
c) a puffer fish

5. Which of these animals can shoot out hot spray?
a) a starfish
b) a bombardier beetle
c) an opossum

Glossary

acid liquid that burns

Antarctic area around the South Pole of Earth

camouflage change in natural colouring or form that makes an animal match its surroundings

defence fighting back to stop an attack

gland part of the body that makes and gives off chemicals

invisible unable to be seen

kidneys pair of bean-shaped organs near the spine that give off waste products

moisture damp, containing liquid

poison substance that can cause death or harm

predator animal that hunts other animals

shed get rid of

Find out more

Books

Animal Encyclopedia (Dorling Kindersley, 2008)

Animals (Record Breakers), Daniel Gilpin (Wayland, 2010)

Penguins, Emily Bone (Usborne, 2009)

Websites

http://animal.discovery.com/videos/fooled-by-nature-horned-lizard.html
http://dsc.discovery.com/videos/nasty-by-nature-horned-lizard-blood-gun.html
Watch a horned lizard in action on these websites. (You may need to watch an advert before the horned lizard videos begin.)

kids.nationalgeographic.com/kids/animals/creaturefeature/emperor-penguin/
Find out about emperor penguins and their superpowers on this website.

Index

Answers: 1a, 2b, 3a, 4c, 5b.

32